NATIVE AMERICAN PEOPLES

INVESTIGATE!

THE HOPI

BY JOHN O'MARA

Enslow
PUBLISHING

Please visit our website, www.enslow.com. For a free color catalog of all our high-quality books, call toll free 1-800-398-2504 or fax 1-877-980-4454.

Library of Congress Cataloging-in-Publication Data
Library of Congress Cataloging-in-Publication Data
Names: O'Mara, John, author.
Title: The Hopi / John O'Mara.
Description: New York : Enslow Publishing, [2022] | Series: Native American peoples | Includes index.
Identifiers: LCCN 2020033612 (print) | LCCN 2020033613 (ebook) | ISBN 9781978521889 (library binding) | ISBN 9781978521865 (paperback) | ISBN 9781978521872 (set) | ISBN 9781978521896 (ebook)
Subjects: LCSH: Hopi Indians–History–Juvenile literature. | Hopi Indians–Social life and customs–Juvenile literature. | Indians of North America–Arizona–History–Juvenile literature.
Classification: LCC E99.H7 O43 2022 (print) | LCC E99.H7 (ebook) | DDC 979.1004/97458–dc23
LC record available at https://lccn.loc.gov/2020033612
LC ebook record available at https://lccn.loc.gov/2020033613

Published in 2022 by
Enslow Publishing
29 E. 21st Street
New York, NY 10010

Copyright © 2022 Enslow Publishing

Designer: Katelyn E. Reynolds
Interior Layout: Tanya Dellaccio
Editor: Therese Shea

Photo credits: Cover, p. 1 (texture) aopsan/Shutterstock.com; cvr, pp. 1–24 (striped texture) Eky Studio/Shutterstock.com; pp. 5 (left), 6 Robert Alexander/Archive Photos/Getty Images; pp. 5 (right), 19 (top right) Bettmann/Getty Images; pp. 7 (both), 17 (left) Werner Forman/Universal Images Group/Getty Images; p. 9 (top left) crossroadscreative/DigitalVision Vectors/Getty Images; pp. 9 (bottom left), 9 (right), 23 (right) Universal History Archive/Universal Images Group/Getty Images; p. 10 Underwood Archives/Archive Photos/Getty Images; p. 11 (left) Hulton Archive/Getty Images; pp. 11 (right), 19 (bottom right) Library of Congress/Corbis Historical/Getty Images; pp. 13 (left), 25 (left) MPI/Archive Photos/Getty Images; pp. 13 (right), 19 (left) Historical/Corbis Historical/Getty Images; p. 14 ClassicStock/Archive Photos/Getty Images; p. 15 https://upload.wikimedia.org/wikipedia/commons/b/bf/Hopi_maiden_wearing_rich_silver_jewelry_and_wampum%2C_Arizona%2C_1898_%28CHS-4603%29.jpg; p. 17 (right) Three Lions/Hulton Archive/Getty Images; p. 20 REDA&CO/Universal Images Group/Getty Images; p. 21 Geoffrey Clements/Corbis Historical/Getty Images; p. 23 (left) Wolfgang Kaehler/LightRocket/Getty Images; pp. 25 (right), 29 Education Images/Universal Images Group/Getty Images; p. 26 AFP/Getty Images; p. 27 https://upload.wikimedia.org/wikipedia/en/a/aa/Oraibi264.jpg; p. 28 Robert Alexander/Archive Photos/Getty Images.

Portions of this work were originally authored by Therese Shea and published as *The Hopi People*. All new material this edition authored by John O'Mara.

All rights reserved. No part of this book may be reproduced in any form without permission in writing from the publisher, except by a reviewer.

Printed in the United States of America

CPSIA compliance information: Batch #CSENS22: For further information contact Enslow Publishing, New York, New York, at 1-800-398-2504.

CONTENTS

A Lasting Culture 4
Interesting Ancestors 6
Hopi Settlement 8
Farmers First 10
Hopi Houses 12
How They Dressed 14
Clans and Villages 16
Young Hopi 18
Religion 20
In the Kiva 22
The Hopi Reservation 24
Resistance 26
Respect the Hopi 28
Glossary 30
For More Information 31
Index 32

WORDS IN THE GLOSSARY APPEAR IN BOLD TYPE THE FIRST TIME THEY ARE USED IN THE TEXT.

A Lasting Culture

The Hopi (HOH-pee) are one of the world's oldest **cultures**. They have lived on the same lands at least as far back as 500 CE. The Hopi people belong to a group of native peoples called the Pueblo. The Pueblo are named for their permanent, or lasting, settlements called pueblos. The Hopi are the westernmost Pueblo. They live mostly in today's Arizona.

The Hopi have fought hard to stay connected to their ancient ways of life. They continue to practice and honor many of their **traditions** hundreds of years later.

GET THE FACTS!

In the Hopi language, *hopi* means "peaceful person." This native people were once called *Moki* by other peoples, a word which means "dead" in the Hopi language. However, it's believed that they didn't give themselves this name.

HOPI WOMEN WERE KNOWN FOR WEARING THEIR HAIR LIKE THIS BEFORE MARRIAGE. THE TRADITION IS STILL CARRIED ON BY SOME.

INTERESTING ANCESTORS

The **ancestors** of Native Americans are believed to have come from eastern Asia more than 12,000 years ago. They likely walked over land between Asia and North America. This land is now covered by water. Then these peoples moved in all directions. Some settled in the desert that's now the southwestern United States. They became farmers and built canals, or man-made waterways, to water their crops.

ANCESTRAL PUEBLO CARVINGS IN ARIZONA

HISTORIANS BELIEVE ABOUT 100 PEOPLE LIVED IN CLIFF PALACE, SHOWN AT LEFT AND BELOW. ANCESTRAL PUEBLO USED STONES FROM RIVERS AS WELL AS WOODEN BEAMS IN THEIR CONSTRUCTION.

GET THE FACTS!

The Ancestral Pueblo built homes within cliffs. They lived in them between 600 and 1300 CE. The most famous are at Mesa Verde National Park in Colorado. The largest cliff dwelling, Cliff Palace, had nearly 200 rooms.

Ancestral Pueblo are thought to be the ancestors of the Hopi. The Hopi call them Hisatsinom (ee-SAH-tse-nom), which means "ancient people."

HOPI SETTLEMENT

Some Ancestral Pueblo moved further south into today's Arizona. Their **descendants** became the Hopi. A Hopi community called Oraibi is likely the oldest **continuously** inhabited, or lived in, village in the United States. It was settled around 1050.

In the 1600s, Spanish people arrived to spread the Christian **religion** to the Hopi. The Spanish also wanted to live in what they called their new territory. Most Hopi didn't accept the new culture. They and other Pueblo peoples drove out the Spanish in 1680. However, the Spanish returned a few years later.

ARIZONA

At left, you can see the location of today's Hopi **reservation**. Below are photos of Oraibi, taken around 1900.

GET THE FACTS!

Many wonder why the Ancestral Pueblo moved from their cliff dwellings. Some think a long drought, or period without rain, forced them to look for water. Others think fights with native groups may have caused the journey south.

FARMERS FIRST

The Hopi raised crops in their dry desert lands. Their main food was corn. They also grew beans, squash, sunflowers, and other vegetables and fruits. The Hopi became herders after getting sheep and other livestock from the Spanish.

GET THE FACTS!

The Hopi grew at least 24 kinds of corn! They knew which kinds to grow in different conditions. Some kinds had roots that reached deep underground to find water. One common Hopi food was a thin cornbread called piki (PEE-kee).

THE HOPI PRACTICED DRY FARMING. THIS KIND OF FARMING DEPENDS ONLY ON RAIN AND SNOW TO WATER CROPS.

Hopi men did the farming and herding. They made blankets and clothing. Hopi women had many jobs too. They made baskets and **pottery**, cooked food, raised the children, and cared for the elderly. They also carried water to their families. This was a hard but important job in the desert.

HOPI HOUSES

The Hopi men built houses for their community too. Hopi houses were made of stone and adobe. Adobe is a mix of earth and straw baked into hard bricks. Adobe kept the house cool in the summer and warm in the winter. Homes were connected, like in an apartment building. Each family had an upstairs and downstairs with several rooms. The downstairs was mostly used for storage. The upstairs was the main living area.

Some traditional Hopi houses are still used today. Other Hopi families live in modern homes and apartment buildings.

HOPI VILLAGES

FIRST MESA
- WALPI
- TEWA
- SITCHUMOVI

SECOND MESA
- SHUNGOPAVI
- MISHONGNOVI
- SIPAULOVI

THIRD MESA
- HOTEVILLA
- BACAVI
- KYKOTSMOVI
- ORAIBI
- UPPER AND LOWER MOENKOPI (PART OF THE THIRD MESA BUT LOCATED WEST OF THE MESA)

GET THE FACTS!

The Hopi lived in desert areas that are marked by mesas. Mesas are like flat-topped mountains or hills with steep sides. (*Mesa* means "table" in Spanish.) Today, Hopi still live on and in the valleys between three mesas, in 12 villages.

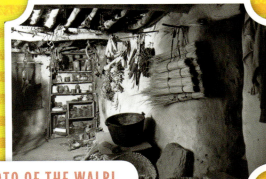

AT LEFT IS A PHOTO OF THE WALPI VILLAGE AROUND 1950. A STORAGE ROOM IS SHOWN AT RIGHT.

HOW THEY DRESSED

The Hopi's clothing kept them cool in the hot desert. Men wore a **breechcloth**. Women wore a knee-length dress called a manta. It joined at one shoulder. Both wore shoes called moccasins made of deerskin. In colder weather, the Hopi wore blankets and leggings to keep warm. Hopi clothing changed over time.

A HOPI MAN PREPARES FOR A SPECIAL EVENT IN THE VILLAGE OF WALPI AROUND 1897.

GET THE FACTS!

The Hopi began to wear silver earrings, bracelets, and rings in the late 1800s. Some say they learned to work metal from the Spanish. Others say a Zuni man named Lanyade taught them. Today, Hopi are famous for their silver jewelry.

Before Hopi women were married, they wore their hair specially placed over their ears. After they were married, they wore two long braids. Hopi men usually wore their hair in a bun. They tied a cloth band around their head.

CLANS AND VILLAGES

The Hopi lived in groups called clans. A clan is made up of a number of families. However, the Hopi thought of their clan as one family. When a Hopi man married, he became part of his wife's clan. Many clans made up a village. Each village had a leader called a kikmongwi. Today's kikmongwis are mainly religious leaders.

The Hopi belonged to societies that had certain duties to perform, such as carrying out **ceremonies**. All men belonged to at least two societies. There were societies just for women too.

BOARD USED IN CEREMONIES BY A HOPI WOMEN'S SOCIETY

GET THE FACTS!

When it was time for a Hopi man or woman to marry, they couldn't choose someone to marry within their own clan. Today, there are 34 clans living in the 12 Hopi villages. Two are the Bear and Parrot clans.

THIS HOPI WOMAN, MINA LANSA, WAS THE KIKMONGWI OF ORAIBI IN THE 1960s.

NUMBER OF HOPI CLANS TODAY: 34

YOUNG HOPI

After Hopi babies were born, they stayed indoors for 19 days. They were placed in a blanket near ears of corn. On the twentieth day, the baby was named during a sunrise ceremony.

Hopi children played with toys, like all children. Girls received dolls as gifts, while boys received bows and arrows. By playing with these, they prepared for roles as mothers and hunters. The children also did chores, or jobs. Boys learned to hunt, grow crops, and make cloth. Girls learned to grind corn, bake bread, and make pottery.

GET THE FACTS!

Even though a husband joined his wife's clan, his old clan had a part to play when the couple had a child. The mother and child were cared for by elders in the father's clan. That clan also named the baby.

These photos from the late 1800s and early 1900s show some roles in Hopi society, including raising children and weaving.

RELIGION

The Hopi religion is **complex**. Some ceremonies are done in secret from outsiders. Hopi religious beliefs include many gods and spirits. Katsinam are invisible, or unseen, spirits of life.

In one known ceremony, Hopi dress in masks to sing and dance in order to honor katsinam. The dancers believe the spirits enter them if the ceremony is done correctly. Traditionally, katsinam were said to bring rain for the crops.

THE HOPI HAVE MANY RELIGIOUS TRADITIONS. OUTSIDERS DON'T KNOW ALL THEIR BELIEFS.

GET THE FACTS!

The Hopi believed that the spirits of dead Hopi people went west to become katsinam. They would return to the community as clouds. It was said that katsinam came to the villages for just half the year, when the Hopi performed ceremonies.

KATSINA DOLLS

The Hopi also made katsina dolls to teach the young about the many spirits. Pueblo peoples recognized more than 500 katsina spirits.

IN THE KIVA

Some of the Hopi religious traditions that we don't know about happen in an underground room called a kiva. Hopi kivas are often square and painted with holy figures or scenes on the walls.

One of the most famous Hopi traditions is the Snake Dance, which takes place in August. Hopi gather live snakes. They wash them and pray with them in the kiva. Some dance with the snakes and then set them free. The dance is a way to give thanks and ask for good fortune.

Hopi artist Fred Kabotie painted the scenes below. They show stories of Hopi ancestors.

SNAKE DANCE

GET THE FACTS!

U.S. president Theodore Roosevelt watched the Snake Dance in 1913. He was allowed into the kiva, which is an honor given to few. Today, people who aren't Hopi cannot watch the Snake Dance. The Hopi people thought outsiders acted too disrespectfully in the past.

THE HOPI RESERVATION

The Hopi way of life changed after Europeans arrived in their lands. It changed more and more as the years went on. In 1848, the United States won a war against Mexico. The nation gained territory, including Hopi lands. In 1882, President Chester A. Arthur created a small Hopi reservation.

For a time, Hopi children were forced to go to schools away from their families. There, they learned English. They were made to dress and act differently than their traditional ways. Sadly, many children became sick at the schools. Some died.

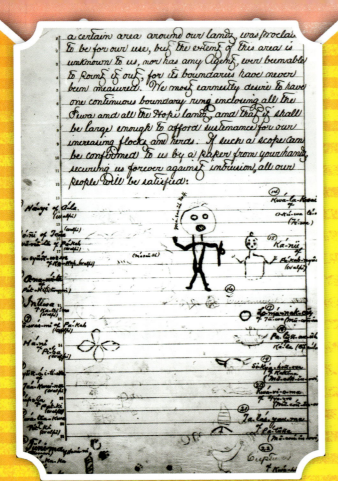

THIS IS PART OF THE 1894 LETTER SENT TO THE U.S. GOVERNMENT ASKING THAT THE HOPI CONTINUE TO FARM AS THEY WISHED.

GET THE FACTS!

The Dawes Act of 1887 required Native Americans to divide their reservation land into lots for each family. The Hopi refused. They sent a message to the U.S. government telling them that their way of farming required shared land.

SHEEP HERD ON HOPI RESERVATION

RESISTANCE

Most Hopi continued to **resist** the changes the U.S. government required of them. In 1894, 19 Hopi were sent to prison for not allowing their children to go to white schools. Sometimes, accepting white ways caused Hopi to fight each other.

HOPI CHILDREN PLAY NEAR THE VILLAGE OF ORAIBI ON THE THIRD MESA OF THE HOPI RESERVATION IN THIS PHOTO FROM AROUND 1970.

GET THE FACTS!

The Hopi Reservation is surrounded by the Navajo Reservation. There are still arguments about land rights between the two peoples. In 1996, the U.S. government granted land to Hopi that Navajo had lived on for a long time.

HOPI RESERVATION

In 1934, the Indian Reorganization Act allowed Native Americans to form their own governments. The Hopi Tribal Council was formed in 1936. The Hopi began to be left alone to continue their traditions as they wanted. Many today are raised in their religion and learn both the English and Hopi languages.

RESPECT THE HOPI

The Hopi welcome visitors to their lands. However, they ask for respect at all times. They don't allow photos or recording on Hopi land. They ask for visitors to open their eyes and hearts to learn about Hopi ways. In some areas, a Hopi guide shows visitors around.

ABOUT 9,000 PEOPLE LIVE IN THE HOPI VILLAGES TODAY.

HOPI RESERVATION SIGN

GET THE FACTS!
Some Hopi make a living by selling crafts, such as pottery and dolls. Some sell from their homes. However, the Hopi Cultural Center on Second Mesa sells Hopi goods. It also instructs visitors how to explore the reservation in a respectful manner.

Hopi work hard to honor their traditions in a changing world. Many still do the hard work of farming on dry land. Hopi have had to fight for the right to the water beneath their lands too. This amazing people know how to survive.

GLOSSARY

ancestor A relative who lived long before you.

breechcloth A cloth that covers the hips.

ceremony An event to honor or celebrate something.

complex Hard to explain or having to do with something with many parts that work together.

continuously In a manner without a break or interruption.

culture The beliefs and ways of life of a group of people.

descendant A person who comes after another in a family.

pottery Objects made of clay that are molded and baked to harden.

religion A belief in and way of honoring a god or gods.

reservation Land set aside by the U.S. government for Native Americans.

resist To oppose or prevent something.

tradition A long-practiced custom.

FOR MORE INFORMATION

BOOKS

Bankston, John. *The Hopi*. Kennett Square, PA: Purple Toad Publishing, Inc., 2020.

Bodden, Valerie. *Hopi*. Mankato, MN: Creative Education, 2020.

Poleahla, Anita. *Celebrate My Hopi Corn*. Flagstaff, AZ: Salina Bookshelf, Inc., 2016.

WEBSITES

Native American Facts for Kids
jan.ucc.nau.edu/hcpo-p/FactsForKids.pdf
Find out more about Hopi culture.

Pueblo Indian History
www.crowcanyon.org/EducationProducts/pueblo_history_kids/introduction.asp
Read about the native group called the Pueblo.

Publisher's note to educators and parents: Our editors have carefully reviewed these websites to ensure that they are suitable for students. Many websites change frequently, however, and we cannot guarantee that a site's future contents will continue to meet our high standards of quality and educational value. Be advised that students should be closely supervised whenever they access the internet.

INDEX

Arizona, 4, 8
children, 11, 18, 19, 24, 26
clans, 16, 17, 19
Cliff Palace, 7
clothing, 11, 14
corn, 10, 18
Dawes Act of 1887, 25
farming, 6, 10, 11, 25, 29
hair, 5, 15
herding, 10, 11
Indian Reorganization Act, 27
katsinam, 20, 21
kikmongwi, 16, 17
kiva, 22, 23
mesas, 13, 29
Navajo, 27
Oraibi, 8, 9, 13, 17, 26
pottery, 11, 18, 29
Pueblo, 4, 7, 8, 9, 21
religion, 8, 16, 20, 27
reservation, 9, 24, 25, 26, 27, 29
silver, 15
Snake Dance, 22, 23
societies, 16